NICK FAV

Unwrapping the seasons
All-age talks for Lent,
Holy Week and Easter

Kevin
Mayhew

First published in 2001 by
KEVIN MAYHEW LTD
Buxhall, Stowmarket, Suffolk, IP14 3BW
Email: info@kevinmayhewltd.com

The material in this book first appeared in *Getting It Across.*

9 8 7 6 5 4 3 2 1 0

ISBN 1 84003 827 6
Catalogue Number 1500460

Front cover design by Angela Selfe
Illustrations by Graham Johnstone
Typesetting by Richard Weaver
Printed and bound in Great Britain

Contents

Introduction

I will never forget the day at Bristol College when I received the orders of service prior to my first preaching engagement and saw leaping out at me two words: Children's Talk. Clearly this was viewed as an integral part of the service, but what exactly was expected of me, still less how I could deliver it, I had no idea. My experience in talking to children was, to say the least, limited, and there was little I had learned up to that point which had prepared me for the task. Had I but known it, no formal training was to be offered in this field anyway, the learning process essentially consisting of being thrown in at the deep end.

I squirm with embarrassment when I look back on some of the early 'children's talks' I delivered, the content simplistic if not downright patronising. Numerous congregations must have exercised enormous patience as slowly I developed my technique at their expense. Yet, strangely, the person who taught me more about the art of successful communication than anyone else was not a member of any one of these congregations, nor one of my college tutors, but an elocutionist I saw for a few brief sessions during my time at Bristol College. His advice consisted of three simple tips:

- always begin by asking a question or using an illustration which involves your audience in what you are saying;
- always end with a simple challenge or question which puts in a nut-shell everything you have been trying to say;
- keep the middle short, simple and to the point.

In every address I have given since then I have kept that advice in mind, not following it slavishly but attempting to apply the essential principles whenever possible. They have stood me in good stead. While I have never considered myself a particularly gifted preacher, still less a natural communicator, the talks I have given throughout my ministry seem generally to have been well received. Why? Partly perhaps because my sermons were always short, but most of all, I believe, because listeners could always find something to relate to.

Having said that, every talk is different. The style of a sermon is quite unlike that of a lecture – at least it should be! The style of a wedding address is nothing like that of a funeral oration. Similarly, the style of a children's talk – or family talk, as I prefer to call it – is totally different again. When young people are present in church you are immediately talking to a wide age-range, spanning two, three or even four generations. It is essential not to talk down to children, and equally important that adults get something more from the talk than a pleasant sense of indulgence. This is all the more important if my suspicion is correct that many adults actually prefer listening to a family-type talk than a sermon, the latter often pitched so far over their heads that their thoughts soon wander to such matters as the state of their Sunday lunch or yesterday's football results!

So what makes a successful family talk? There is no one answer to that, but for me the following are all vital ingredients:

- an element of fun
- appropriate visual aids
- 'audience' participation
- all-age relevance
- brief applications
- thorough preparation
- attractive presentation

Let me deal with each of these in turn.

Fun

With any audience a little light-heartedness goes a long way towards establishing a rapport. When talking to young people this becomes all the more essential, as there are so many other attractions in our society competing for their time. Too often I have attended services in which the 'talk to the children' is little more than a mini (or not so mini) sermon, and the ineffectiveness of this approach has been eloquently testified to by scarcely suppressed expressions of boredom. Not only do such talks fail to get the message across but, far worse, they effectively drive young people away from our churches.

Visual Aids

My own preference has always been to include some sort of visual aid in a talk, even if this is simply key words stuck to a board. Indeed, words and words games, as you will see, figure prominently throughout this book. It is a fact that what we see stays in our minds far longer than what we simply hear.

Audience Participation

Young people (and many older ones too) like to be involved in a 'learning process' rather than simply being talked to. Games, word-searches, quizzes and other such forms of participation offer an effective way of including the congregation in what you are saying. We need to promote an atmosphere in which people feel part of what is going on.

All-age Relevance

As I have said already, many adults are actually far more receptive to a talk geared towards a younger audience than they are to a sermon.

Many also enjoy participation as much as children, if not more so! Even if this were not the case, we owe it to any congregation to ensure that a talk is able both to stimulate and challenge.

Brief Applications

I have always believed that the secret of a successful family talk is to keep the application – the serious bit at the end – as short and simple as possible. Ideally, the message you are looking to put across (and this ought to be *one* message, not several) should speak for itself through the illustrations and visual aids you use, though some expansion of what this means is usually necessary. Overdo the application and you will pay the price. Which of us hasn't witnessed the sudden glazed looks the moment the 'religious' part of a talk is reached. Whatever you do, don't try and ram the point home; if you haven't made the point through the fun part of your talk, you won't make it afterwards.

Thorough Preparation

There is no getting away from it: talking to young people takes time. There were many occasions during my ministry when I spent longer preparing a single family talk (even one lasting a mere five minutes) than two full-length sermons. In this book I have attempted to do most of the spadework for you through suggesting ideas and ways of presenting these, but to deliver most of the talks you will still need to spend some time in preparation. Don't be put off by this. The effort may occasionally seem out of proportion to the time taken up by the talk during the service, but I believe the results will more than justify it. What you put in, you will get out.

Attractive Presentation

In this sophisticated age, young people as much as adults are used to slick, glossy and professional presentations. While we cannot emulate these, it is important for visual material to be as clear and well presented as possible. The advent of the home computer makes this far easier to achieve than it once was, as well as saving huge amounts of time. While material can be written out by hand (for many of these talks I did just that), I would strongly recommend the use of a PC word-processing package if possible.

When it comes to displaying material, my own preference, arrived at after several years of trial and error, is to use a magnetic whiteboard in conjunction with magnetic tape (available through most office stationery suppliers), with the back-up of a second whiteboard (magnetic or otherwise) and Blu-Tack. You will also need easels for these, as light and portable as possible. A supply of thick coloured marker pens (in washable and permanent ink) is a must for many talks, as is a copious supply of thin card and/or paper. Several of the talks could be delivered using an overhead projector and screen if this is preferred to board and easel. Adapt to your available resources.

On a purely practical note, make use of a radio microphone if this is available. Family talks often involve a degree of movement, and it is all too easy to stray from a standing microphone so that you become inaudible, or, worse still, to trip headlong over the wires of a halter neck model! (The younger members of the congregation will delight in this, but for you it can prove embarrassing and even dangerous.)

Each talk in this collection is set out according to a basic framework:

- a suggested Bible passage which should normally be read publicly prior to the talk
- a statement of the aim of the talk
- details of preparation needed beforehand
- the talk itself.

This last section includes instructions relating, for example, to the use of illustrations, together with a suggested application of the talk. The talks will work best if, having read and digested these paragraphs, you present them in your own words. This is particularly true where the congregation is invited to respond, and developing and incorporating their ideas and answers into the talk will require a measure of ad-libbing on your part.

Each of the talks in this booklet have been used in public worship during my time in the ministry. No doubt many are flawed in places and could be considerably improved – I do not offer them as examples of how it should be done, but rather as a resource which may be of help to you. Of all the comments received during my ministry, few have gratified me more than those when young people have referred in conversation to talks I delivered three, four, even five years back. Whether they remembered the point I had been making I cannot say, but whatever else they had enjoyed being in church and carried away positive associations of their time there. That in itself was always sufficient motivation to spend further time and energy devoted to getting the message across.

Nick Fawcett

LENT

1   Confessing

Reading   Psalm 32:1-11

Aim   To remind us that Lent is a time of challenge, urging us to confess our faults, but also a time of hope, bringing the promise of forgiveness.

Preparation   On pieces of card, or paper, print the following words or part-words:

CONFESSING
(print this horizontally and display on the centre of a board)

A   (print these vertically – see **Talk** below)
QUIT
ABS
LVE
PARDO
ORGIVE
M
RCY
HRIVE
ORRY
ADM
T
REPE
TANCE
APOLO
ISE

Fix magnetic tape or Blu-Tack to the back of each.

Talk   Tell the congregation that you have prepared a short quiz designed to help explain the meaning of Lent. One of the traditions of the Church over the centuries has been to begin Lent by confessing one's faults and seeking forgiveness. The aim of the quiz is to discover what 'confessing' actually means, and each of the answers will have at least one letter of the word 'confessing' in it. As each correct response is given, arrange the appropriate parts of the word as set out below.

1. What word means to pronounce someone not guilty?
2. What word means to pronounce forgiveness?
3. What do we beg if we've done something wrong?
4. What do we ask God to do to our trespasses in the Lord's Prayer?
5. What do we show to someone if we let them off punishment?
6. What word meaning to cleanse is associated with last Tuesday?
7. What do we say if we have done something wrong?

8. What word means own up to?

9. What did John the Baptist call people to before being baptised?

10. What word means to say sorry?

```
                        P                                       A
                        A                           R           P
              A         R                   A       E           O
              B         D                   D       P           L
    A         S         O         M         M       E           O
    C    O    N    F    E    S    S    I    N    G
    Q    L         O    R    H    O    T    T         I
    U    V         R    C    R    R         A         S
    I    E         G    Y    I    R         N         E
    T              I         V    Y         C
                   V         E              E
                   E
```

Today is the first day/Sunday of Lent: a time for CONFESSING everything that is wrong in our lives; a time in which we need to ADMIT our mistakes and show true REPENTANCE through saying SORRY and APOLOGISING to God.

But it is also a time for remembering that God is ready to FORGIVE us, a time for rejoicing in his MERCY and PARDON. It is a time which reminds us that, through the grace of Christ, he is ready to ACQUIT and ABSOLVE – or, as the old English word puts it, SHRIVE – us of all we have done wrong.

This, then, is what Lent is all about; a time of challenge but also promise, summed up in the words of Psalm 32:

I acknowledged my sin to you, and I did not hide my iniquity; I said, 'I will confess my transgressions to the Lord,' and you forgave the guilt of my sin. *(Psalm 32:5)*

Thanks be to God!

2 Multiple choice

Reading Luke 4:1-12

Aim To demonstrate that choices are not always easy, and the right way is not always as clear as we would like, but if we seek God's guidance he will help us choose wisely.

Preparation The only preparation needed is to print the three alternative spellings for 'Commitment' (see below). You may, however, like to print all the questions for visual effect.

Talk Tell the congregation that you have prepared a simple quiz for Lent, with a mixture of easy and not-so-easy questions. Invite volunteers to suggest answers.

GENERAL KNOWLEDGE
- What is the highest mountain in the world? *(Everest)*
- How much is 25 divided by 5? *(5)*
- What colour do you get if you mix yellow and red? *(Orange)*
- Who won the FA Cup last year? *(Make sure you know the answer!)*

TRUE OR FALSE:
- A rolling stone gathers no moss *(True)*
- 4 + 4 = 9 *(False)*
- Henry VIII had six wives *(True)*
- You shall love your neighbour as yourself *(As Christians, we believe that's true)*

MULTIPLE CHOICE
- What is the capital of Canada: (1) Toronto, (2) Ontario, or (3) Ottawa? *(Ottawa)*
- How many horns does an Indian rhinoceros have: (1) none, (2) one, or (3) two? *(Two)*
- Which spelling is correct: (1) Committment, (2) Commitment, or (3) Comitment? *(Commitment)*
- What is the speed of sound: (1) 240 mph, (2) 760 mph, or (3) 980 mph? *(760 mph)*

There were three different kinds of question in the quiz: some where the answer was obvious; others which called for a choice between three possible answers; others still where the answer depended on personal convictions about right and wrong! And that mixture of questions was chosen for a purpose, because in life we are faced in much the same way with different kinds of choices. Sometimes a course of action is clearly right or wrong. Sometimes we may be faced with a variety of options, and we have to choose which one is right. And sometimes the choice we make is down to what we believe – a question of faith.

Choices, then, are not always easy, but when we are faced with the need to choose we should look back to the forty days Jesus faced in the wilderness; for at the end of that time he too was faced with difficult choices – the need to choose between good and bad, right and wrong! There were three very different temptations. To bow before Satan, that was clearly wrong. But to turn stones into bread, what was so wrong with that? As for throwing himself off the temple to test God's purpose, couldn't the Bible itself be used to justify this? Complicated but vital choices at the very start of his ministry, which, for Jesus, would affect not only his own future but ours too.

Lent calls us to take a long and hard look at our lives; to consider the choices we have made, and the choices facing us now. The answers may not be easy to find, but if, like Jesus, we are ready to seek God's guidance and listen to his voice, we will find the wisdom we need to choose between what's right and what's wrong.

3   A time to decide

Readings   Ecclesiastes 3:1-8; Matthew 3:1-17

Aim   To make the point that Lent is a time for quiet reflection, but also sometimes for decision; we need to seek God's timing to discover which is right for us.

Preparation   Draw, print from a computer programme, or use pictures from magazines or greetings cards to illustrate the following, and arrange them on a display board:

a person sunbathing
a snowman
a daffodil
a birthday cake
a Christmas tree
wedding bells
a sheaf or an ear of corn/wheat
a (red) rose
a pumpkin
an Easter egg
fireworks

Write or print the following words and arrange them on a separate board:

Harvest
Summer
Easter
Christmas
Birthday
Halloween
Winter
Spring
Valentine's Day
Wedding
Bonfire Night

On strips of card, print the following proverbs in large letters:

Fools rush in
Make haste slowly
Rome wasn't built in a day
Don't bite off more than you can chew
Don't count your chickens before they are hatched
Don't try and run before you can walk
Look before you leap

Procrastination is the thief of time
Make hay while the sun shines
Don't put off to tomorrow what you can do today
Time waits for no man
He who hesitates is lost

Now cut these up so that they can be rearranged as follows:

Fools rush in before they are hatched
He who hesitates waits for no man
Time wasn't built in a day
Make hay today
Don't bite off more than the thief of time
Rome is lost
Don't count your chickens while the sun shines
Don't put off to tomorrow what you can do slowly
Procrastination is in
Look you can chew
Don't try and run before you can leap
Make haste before you can walk

Arrange these jumbled proverbs on the back of one of the display boards.

Talk   Tell the congregation that you have put together some words and pictures designed to help them understand the readings from Ecclesiastes and Matthew. First though, you need their help to match the words to the picture. Ask for suggestions. The answers are as follows:

Sunbathing	Summer
Snowman	Winter
Daffodil	Spring
Cake	Birthday
Tree	Christmas
Bells	Wedding
Wheat	Harvest
Rose	Valentine's Day
Pumpkin	Halloween
Fireworks	Bonfire Night
Easter egg	Easter

With each of these pictures there is clearly a time and a place that fits them all. How many of you, for example, would go sunbathing in winter? Or which of you would attempt to build a snowman in the middle of summer? The very idea is ridiculous!

And it is just this that the writer of the book of Ecclesiastes was emphasising in those words we heard earlier: there is a right time for everything, no matter what it may be. True though that is, unfortunately it is sometimes not always as obvious when that right time actually is.

Take, for example, this list of proverbs. (Turn over the display board to reveal the jumbled proverbs prepared beforehand. Read them through as they stand, then invite the congregation to help arrange them as they should be.)

These proverbs, in different ways, are all concerned with time. Some warn of the danger of doing things too quickly, deciding on a course of action before we've had time to think the implications through properly. Others warn about the danger of failing to decide, putting off a decision until it is too late. We have to tread a fine balance between those two extremes. Whenever we have an important decision to make it's important to think about it carefully, but equally the time comes when we must decide. And that is precisely what happened to Jesus when he heard that John the Baptist was preaching and baptising in the wilderness; he knew that the time had come for him to decide.

> Then Jesus came from Galilee to the Jordan to be baptised by John. But John tried to deter him, saying, 'I need to be baptised by you, and do you come to me?' Jesus replied, 'Let it be so now; it is proper for us to do this to fulfil all righteousness.'
> (Matthew 3:13)

Up until then, Jesus had been waiting for the right moment; making haste slowly, rather than rushing in. Eighteen years had passed since he had gone to the temple with his parents, and often he must have wondered how much longer he would have to wait before he began the ministry to which God had called him. But the time was not right until John had prepared the way, and it was only then that Jesus knew the time had come to begin his ministry – to respond to God's call and offer his life. Suddenly *now* was the time to act, the time to decide, the time to respond, and there could be no hesitating or putting it off. A new chapter in his life was about to start.

What is God calling *us* to? Is he calling us to come to faith in him, and, if so, is it time to stop putting a decision off and make up our minds? Is he calling us to baptism or church membership; is it time to decide, or do we need more time to think things through? Is he calling us to new areas of service, to take on new responsibilities, to attempt new things; or is he challenging us to stop and take stock of where we are and what we are already doing?

Lent is a time for pausing and reflecting upon what God wants from us; a time for listening to his voice and seeking his will. God does not call us to rush into faith or anything else, but when the time is right he expects us to respond. Is he calling you to wait and think further before you make up your mind? Or is he saying to you, firmly but unmistakably, now is the time to decide?

4   The price is right!

Reading   Mark 8:34-35; 14:3-9

Aim   To emphasise the fact that following Jesus involves cost as well as reward, but that the greatness of his love, beyond all price, deserves a fitting response.

Preparation   Buy three items of confectionery (a packet of Maltesers, a tube of Smarties, a bar of chocolate, for example). Keep a note of how much each item cost.

Prepare three sets of four large eye-catching cards with a different price on each (for example, 26p, 27p, 28p, 29p). Ensure that in each set the correct price is included. The prices should be relatively close to each other, rather than clearly too high or too low.

You will also need nine pieces of blank card and three marker pens for use by your volunteers.

Talk   Tell the congregation that you are going to play your own version of the popular television game, *The price is right!* Ask for volunteers, and select three contestants to 'come on down!'. Give each of the contestants a marker pen and three pieces of card. Hold up the first item and then, after displaying the four prices, ask them to write down which price they think you actually paid.

After each round hold up the card with the right price. At the end of the game give each of the volunteers one of the items of confectionery.

How many guessed right? For those who didn't, it doesn't really matter for we were talking here about a few pence only. But there are times when knowing how much something might cost us is very important, for we need to decide whether or not we are able to afford it. And that is true not only when it comes to money but in other ways too.

Take, for example, the story of the woman who knelt before Jesus and poured a jar of hugely expensive ointment on his feet – a gift of such enormous value that some of those watching complained about the waste of money.

> Why was this ointment wasted in this way? For this ointment could have been sold for more than three hundred denarii, and the money given to the poor. *(Mark 14:4b-5)*

What they said was quite true, but for this woman her gift was a way of offering not just her money but her whole life to Jesus, for in him she had found a meaning to life which was beyond price.

Lent reminds us that we too need to respond to the love of God shown in Jesus, which ultimately led him to death on the cross. Here is a love that we can never begin to repay, but if we are serious about following Jesus, there is a cost involved.

If any want to become my followers, let them deny themselves and take up their cross and follow me. For those who want to save their life will lose it, and those who lose their life for the sake of the gospel, will save it. *(Mark 8:34-35)*

To follow Jesus will mean sometimes letting go of self-interest, denying our own needs and wishes in preference to someone else's, having less so that others may have more.

What is the cost of following Jesus? In a sense the answer is nothing, for the love of God is free to all, offered by grace alone. But if we truly love Jesus and are serious about following him, then we will want to repay his love through offering our service. There is a price to discipleship, but it is a price worth paying, for it leads to lasting happiness and life in all its fullness.

5   It's your choice

Reading   Luke 5:1-11, 27-28

Aim   To illustrate the message that Lent is about choices – not just those Jesus had to make during his temptation in the wilderness, but the choices we have to make every day of our lives.

Preparation   You will need a small selection of sweets, a coin, three or four straws (one shorter than the others), and a dice.

Talk   Tell the congregation that you have a mouthwatering selection of sweets with which to tempt them. Invite volunteers to come forward, and explain that before they can choose a sweet they must first make another simple choice. Make the right decision, and a sweet is theirs.

Choices can be made as follows, or using ideas of your own:

- Conceal a coin in one hand, and ask which hand it's in.
- Hold up your collection of straws, and ask who can draw the short straw.
- Throw the dice, and ask volunteers to guess which number will come up.
- Ask a straightforward true or false question. For example, Luke was a fisherman: true or false?
- Ask a multiple choice question. For example, the other name given in the Bible to Levi is (a) Simon, (b) Matthew, or (c) Philip?

What has all this to do with the reading from Luke's Gospel. The answer is simple: it was up to the volunteers to come to their own decision. No one forced them to come forward and take part; no one influenced their choice as they made their decision – it was up to them.

The same was true for Peter, James and John. When Jesus first called them, there was no pressure. He didn't insist on joining them; he asked if he could. He didn't force them to carry on fishing; he encouraged them to throw out their nets one last time. He didn't compel them to become his disciples; he invited them to follow. The final decision was theirs, no one else's.

And so it is with us. God has given us free will. He offers guidance through the Scriptures, he shows us how to live through the example of Jesus, but he never twists our arms. We have a choice: our way or his; to live for ourselves or live for him; self-interest or self-sacrifice? Lent calls us to think about the choices before us, and to decide which path we will take.

6   Which way now?

Reading Matthew 7:3-14 (to be read at the end of the talk rather than before it)

Aim To bring home the fact that following Jesus sometimes involves difficult but important choices on which our future depends.

Preparation On a large sheet of card, or directly on to a whiteboard, prepare for a game of Hangman by drawing dashes to represent each letter of the following:

- The gate that leads to destruction is wide and the way is easy.
- The gate that leads to life is narrow and the way hard.
- Those who find it are few.

You will also need a marker pen to fill in the missing letters as they are guessed (or to draw the 'hanged man').

Talk Tell the congregation that you are challenging them to a game of Hangman, only it is a game with a difference! Instead of guessing one word, they have to guess 31 words, which together summarise two verses from the Bible! Invite people to suggest a letter. (Although identifying 31 words sounds difficult, it is actually easier than identifying a single word – the hard part is for you to fill in all the places where a particular letter fits!)

When the game has been completed, explain that it was all about choices – making the right choices! There were 26 letters to choose from, but, of course, not 26 opportunities to choose them, so you had to make a decision as to the best ones to choose. Similarly, Jesus was reminding his listeners in those words we've just uncovered that life involves the need to choose. What he actually said was this:

'Enter through the narrow gate; for the gate is wide and the road is easy that leads to destruction, and there are many who take it. For the gate is narrow and the road is hard that leads to life, and there are few who take it.' *(Matthew 7:13)*

Just as there were many letters to choose from in the game but only a few right ones, so it is with life in general. There are all kinds of choices we can make, but though some may look appealing they lead us nowhere, or, worse, lead us astray. The way that leads to life is the way that Jesus has shown, but it is a way that involves difficult and sometimes costly choices which we may prefer not to make.

Lent reminds us that Jesus was willing to make such difficult choices himself; taking the way of the cross, of suffering and sacrifice, so great was his love for the world. And that example asks each of us, quite simply, which way will we choose: the way of self-interest and self-service, or the way of self-denial and serving others.

PALM SUNDAY

7 Discovering the kingdom

Reading   Luke 19:29-40

Aim   To show that Jesus is a different type of king, ruling over a different kind of kingdom.

Preparation   From silver or gold card, make thirteen simple crowns, and on the front of each one stick a large label with the name of one of the following:

> Tutankhamen
> Nebuchadnezzar
> Julius Caesar
> James VI
> Henry V
> Louis XIV
> Philip II
> Genghis Khan
> Frederick the Great
> Montezuma
> Nicholas
> Boadicea
> Jesus

Now, on coloured pieces of card or paper, cut out thirteen large contoured shapes, representing countries. On each of these write the name of one of the following countries:

> Egypt
> Babylon
> Rome
> Scotland
> England
> France
> Spain
> Mongolia
> Prussia
> Aztecs (Mexico)
> Russia
> Iceni

Using Blu-Tack, stick these 'countries' around the front of the church, on walls, the lectern and choir stalls.

Talk   Ask the congregation if they have ever wondered what it must be like to be a king? Tell them that, for a few lucky volunteers, today is their opportunity to find out, because for five minutes you are going to give them the chance to rule a country. Ask for thirteen volunteers, give each one a crown to wear, and then ask each 'king' to discover their kingdom and hold it up for all to see. The correct countries are:

Tutankhamen	Egypt
Nebuchadnezzar	Babylon
Julius Caesar	Rome
James VI	Scotland
Henry V	England
Louis XIV	France
Philip II	Spain
Genghis Khan	Mongolia
Frederick the Great	Prussia
Montezuma	Aztecs (Mexico)
Nicholas	Russia
Boadicea	Iceni
Jesus	?

All of your 'kings' should quickly be able to find their kingdoms except for the one whose crown bears the name 'Jesus'. Arrange the 'kings' in a line with 'Jesus' on one end; then, starting at the other end, announce the name on each volunteer's crown and country, and ask whether these have been paired correctly (exchange if necessary). Continue along the line until you reach the volunteer wearing the crown with the name 'Jesus'. Why has no country been found to match?

When Jesus entered Jerusalem on what today we call Palm Sunday, it was to be welcomed as king by the crowds who had gathered there to greet him.

'Blessed is the king who comes in the name of the Lord!', they shouted. *(Luke 19:38)*

So what kind of king was Jesus; and where was, or is, his kingdom? The obvious answer, of course, is that he was king of the Jews, or the king of Israel. And that is exactly what many people at the time hoped he had come to be, what others feared he intended to be, and what the Roman authorities suspected he claimed to be.

Then Pilate asked him, 'Are you the king of the Jews?' *(Luke 23:3)*

But the answer Jesus gave was very different.

'My kingdom is not from this world. If my kingdom were from this world, my followers would be fighting to keep me from being handed over to the Jews. But as it is, my kingdom is not from here.' *(John 18:36)*

Those are words we need to remind ourselves of today. When we talk about Jesus being our king, when we sing hymns with words like 'You are the King of Glory', 'Majesty', or 'Rejoice, the Lord is King', we are not saying he is a king like any of these others we have looked at today. For Jesus was not a king in the sense of ruling a single country many years ago. Rather he came as the servant of all, the one who laid down his life for his people, the one who put others before himself, yet the one raised up by God as ruler over all, the King of kings and Lord of lords, now and for all eternity. Here we glimpse the kind of kingdom God has in store for us and all his people and the sort of king Jesus will be. In the words of the hymn, 'This is our God, the Servant King'.

Finish with the hymn *From heaven you came (The Servant King)*.

8   A surprising side

Reading   John 2:13-25

Aim   From the account of Jesus turning out the traders from the temple in Jerusalem, to show that, while anger is typically a destructive emotion, there are times when it is not only understandable but essential.

Preparation   In large, bold letters print or write the following riddle:

> My first is in WRATH and not found in MEEK.
> My second's in STRONG instead of in WEAK.
> My third is in RAGING and not found in MILD.
> My fourth is in TEMPER and also in RILED.
> My last is in FURY, and also in IRE.
> My whole was displayed by our surprising Messiah!

Display this at the front of the church, allowing time before the talk for people to see it and try to work it out (even if this does mean they are not concentrating on the rest of the service!). Ensure that the Bible passage above has been read prior to this talk.

Talk   Ask if anyone is able to solve the riddle you have set them. As a clue, tell them that the answer describes how Jesus was feeling in the passage of Scripture read earlier. The answer you are looking for, of course, is ANGER. Run through the riddle and explain how you arrive at this answer.

There are some people who think of Jesus as MEEK and MILD, but the story of him turning out the traders from the temple reminds us that there was nothing WEAK about him. When Jesus saw what was going on in the temple – corruption and exploitation being allowed to continue unchecked – he was filled with WRATH, giving vent to his IRE in a RAGING display of TEMPER, the FURY of which took the traders and moneylenders in the temple by surprise.

Here is a side to Jesus we are not used to, and perhaps one which makes us feel a little uncomfortable, the idea that he could be capable of such STRONG feelings when RILED fitting uneasily with the picture we have of him. Yet it is a side we need to recognise and grapple with, for, although nine times out of ten anger is a destructive thing, there are times when it is right to feel angry. When we see injustice around us, when evil triumphs over good, when the innocent are made to suffer, when unnecessary hurt is caused to others – at times like these it is not only right to feel angry, it is imperative: the only response that will do!

HOLY WEEK

9   A heavy load

Readings   Isaiah 53:4-5; Matthew 10:1-15

Aim   To bring home the truth that, whatever problems or troubles may weigh us down, Jesus, through his death on the cross, is able to carry those burdens and so set us free.

Preparation   Get hold of two large identical boxes. Pack one full to the top with the heaviest items you can get hold of – books, cartons of water, lead weights, for example. Pack the other with polystyrene foam.

Talk   Ask if anyone is feeling strong. Tell the congregation you hope someone is, because you need help. You've been busy tidying up the church office and you have two boxes that you need carried to the back of the church ready to take home later. You are happy to take one, but who will help you with the other? Invite volunteers to come forward. Ask the first volunteer to pick up the heavy box, while you pick up the light one. Express astonishment at their inability to pick the box up or carry it. Invite other volunteers to have a go, until everyone who wants to has had a turn. Make a joke of the fact that you never realised you were so strong! Then ask if anyone can explain why you found lifting your box so easy while your volunteers found theirs so hard. Open the boxes and display what's inside.

Imagine if we had to carry a heavy load around with us all the time! We couldn't do it, could we? Yet there is a sense in which we constantly do just that, allowing our lives to become full of problems and anxieties that burden us, fears and doubts that hold us down, or past mistakes and present weaknesses which prevent us living life to the full. All too often we struggle along through life, getting by as best we can, yet feeling increasingly unable to cope.

If that is how you're feeling, then listen again to the wonderful words of Jesus from the Gospel of Matthew:

Come to me, all you that are weary and are carrying heavy burdens, and I will give you rest. Take my yoke upon you, and learn from me; for I am gentle and humble in heart, and you will find rest for your souls. For my yoke is easy, and my burden is light.
(Matthew 11:28-30)

These are words of Jesus spoken not only to his disciples and followers long ago, but to each of us now. For through his life and his death Jesus has carried on his shoulders the burdens we bear. Whatever mistakes we may have made, whatever fears may haunt us, whatever problems may beset us, he has dealt with them on the cross.

In the words of the prophet Isaiah:

> Surely he has borne our infirmities and carried our diseases; yet we accounted him stricken, struck down by God, and afflicted. But he was wounded for our transgressions, crushed for our iniquities; upon him was the punishment that made us whole, and by his bruises we are healed. *(Isaiah 53:4-5)*

For us all, there are times when we feel weighed down by the troubles and difficulties of life, unable sometimes to take another step. But the truth we celebrate today and in the days ahead is that Jesus has taken our burdens upon himself, and is ready to release us from whatever load we bear, setting us free to live life to the full!

Finish with the hymn *Burdens are lifted at Calvary*.

10 The difference a week makes!

Reading Luke 19:28-40

Aim To demonstrate the contrast between the fickleness of human nature and the faithfulness of God, each so powerfully displayed in the events from Palm Sunday to Easter Sunday.

Preparation You will need a large sheet of paper pinned to a board, or a whiteboard, and a marker pen. Across the top of the board write the following:

LOVE   CHEER   WAVE   JOY   PALM   KING

Talk Tell the congregation that you want to talk about change, and to help illustrate what you mean you need their help. Show them the letters at the top of your display board, and tell them that you want to change the words in as few stages as possible to very different words: 'Love' to 'Hate'; 'Cheer' to 'Cross'; 'Wave' to 'Mock'; 'Joy' to 'Woe'; 'Palm' to 'Harm'; and 'King' to 'Kill'. Invite suggestions as how best to do this, and write these down beneath the relevant word until the change has successfully been made. If the ways below are faster (or if you can do better!), demonstrate afterwards.

LOVE	CHEER	WAVE	JOY	PALM	KING
COVE	CHEEP	RAVE	TOY	PALE	PING
CAVE	CHEAP	RACE	TOE	HALE	PINT
HAVE	CHEAT	RACK	WOE	HARE	TINT
HATE	CHEST	ROCK		HARM	TILT
	CREST	MOCK			KILT
	CRESS				KILL
	CROSS				

Point out that in a relatively short time it was possible to change the word you started with into a word very different in meaning. But if changing the words so easily seems remarkable, more remarkable still is the fact that the changes you have made actually happened. What day is it? Palm Sunday. What day will it be next Friday? Good Friday.

Palm Sunday and Good Friday: two very different days reminding us of very different events, yet there is less than a week between them. In less than a week, love changed to hate, cheering changed to a cross, the joyful waving of crowds changed to mockery, the joyful hurling of palm branches turned to the hurling of insults and attempts to harm Jesus, the shouts welcoming him as King turned to shouts demanding he should be killed; a day of joy turned to a day of woe. In just a few days, each of these changes took place.

An astonishing turnaround; but thankfully there was to be another more astonishing still, for on Easter Day Jesus was to change it all back again! Hate was replaced by love, the tears after the cross were replaced by cheers following the Resurrection, the mocking of the crowds gave way to hands waving in happiness, woe was replaced by joy, the one who had been killed was worshipped as Lord of lords and King of kings!

Palm Sunday reminds us how quickly people can change, ourselves included; how short-lived our love and faithfulness can be. But it reminds us also that the love of God shown in Christ never changes; that whatever may fight against his will, and however faithless we may be, his love and purpose will endure for ever!

11   Sign of Christ's presence

Readings   Exodus 12:14-20; Matthew 26:17-29

Aim   To show that Holy Communion is a special meal that speaks powerfully of everything God has done for us in Christ.

Preparation   Print the following on separate strips of card:

Shrove Tuesday	Pancake
Christmas	Christmas pudding
Cream tea	Scone, jam and cream
Good Friday	Hot cross bun
Wedding reception	Wedding cake
Picnic	Cakes and biscuits
Barbecue	Hot dog
Breakfast	Cornflakes
Passover Festival	Bitter herbs
Garden party	Tea and cucumber sandwiches
Birthday party	Jelly and blancmange
McDonald's	Hamburger
Burns' Night	Haggis
Harvest supper	Fruit and vegetables/Bread and wine

Arrange those in the first column down the left-hand side of a display board. With a piece of Blu-Tack stick the items in the second column around the front of the church where they are visible to all. (If you're feeling adventurous, you might consider offering samples of the items in the right-hand column for volunteers to taste.)

Talk   Explain that around the church you have scattered the names of different types of food, all of which might be eaten in different places and at different kinds of meals. Invite volunteers to come forward and match the foods to the occasions on the board (as above).

These occasions are all different meals in which we might share at different times. Some are for celebrating; some are about remembering the past; some are simply a way of sharing socially. But how about the two things left over, bread and wine – when might we use these? The answer, of course, is the occasion we call Holy Communion, or Eucharist, or the Lord's Supper. A simple but special meal, which is not only a way of sharing together but also a way of remembering and celebrating. And in this week, of all weeks, we remember how that meal started, as Jesus shared his last supper with his disciples.

They had gathered together to share in the traditional Jewish celebration of Passover: a meal and a festival at the heart of the Jewish faith.

This day shall be a day of remembrance for you . . . When your children ask you, 'What do you mean by this observance?' you shall say, 'It is the Passover sacrifice to the Lord, for he passed over the houses of the Israelites in Egypt, when he struck down the Egyptians but spared our houses.' *(Exodus 12:14)*

For the Jews this was, and is still, a way of remembering and celebrating all God had done for them, most particularly in delivering them from slavery in Egypt centuries before. It is a meal which unites them as individual families and as a nation, in a common faith.

But there, in a simple upstairs room, and an even simpler meal, Jesus gave this festival a new meaning to his followers. Suddenly it spoke not of what God had done centuries before, but of what he was doing there and then among them. And across the centuries since, this meal of bread and wine has spoken to countless people of what God has done and is still doing in Jesus Christ. It reminds us first that Jesus died for our sakes on the cross:

While they were eating, Jesus took a loaf of bread, and after blessing it he broke it, gave it to his disciples and said, 'Take, eat, this is my body.' *(Matthew 26:26)*

It reminds us also that he rose again and is with us now:

Then they told what had happened, and how Jesus had been made known to them in the breaking of the bread. *(Luke 24:35)*

And it reminds us finally that Jesus will come again to establish his kingdom and rule the earth:

I tell you, I will never again drink of this fruit of the vine until that day when I drink it new with you in my Father's kingdom. *(Matthew 26:27)*

A meal can simply be a time for enjoying food, or for sharing; a time for remembering the past, or for celebrating a special occasion. But this meal, though simpler than any, says more than all, for it is a testimony to God's love and a sign of Christ's presence.

12   The way of humility

Readings   Isaiah 53:1-9; Philippians 2:1-11

Aim   To contrast the way of self-denial exemplified by Jesus with the way of self-interest so often seen in the world.

Preparation   Select some slogans from television advertisements (suggestions are given below, but these will have already begun to date). Arrange the names of the products in a column down the left side of a display board. Print your selected slogans in large, bold letters and attach magnetic tape or Blu-Tack to the back of each, ready for later use.

> Bounty – A taste of paradise
> Carlsberg – Probably the best lager in the world
> Kwik-Fit – You can't fit quicker than a Kwik-Fit fitter
> British Airways – The world's favourite airline
> Flake – Only the crumbliest flakiest chocolate
> Kellogg's – The original and best
> McVities – Bake a better biscuit
> Duracell – Looks like and lasts like no other battery
> Vauxhall – Once driven, forever smitten
> Mars Bar – A Mars a day helps you work rest and play
> Mr Kipling – Makes exceedingly good cakes
> Pedigree Chum – Nine out of ten top breeders recommend it
> Milky Way – The snack you can eat between meals
> McDonald's – A visit to McDonald's makes your day
> Tesco – Every little helps

Talk   Ask the congregation how many of them watch the advertisements on television. Tell them you are going to test today how well these advertisements have achieved their aim. Read through the list of products on the display board, then ask if anyone can match the appropriate slogans to each one. Invite suggestions, and insert the slogan next to the product when the correct answer is given.

Our examples highlight just some of the extravagant boasts advertisers make for the things they sell. Each claims to have the best product on the market. And most of us at some time or other have probably met people rather similar: full of their own importance, convinced they know it all, and looking down their noses at others – the sort of people we might describe as too full of themselves by half! Compare their attitude with the one we see in the reading from Philippians:

> Do nothing from selfish ambition or conceit, but in humility regard others as better than yourselves. Let each of you look not to your own interests, but to the interests of others. Let the same mind be in you that was in Christ Jesus, who, though he was in the

form of God, did not regard equality with God as something to be exploited, but emptied himself, taking the form of a slave, being born in human likeness. And being found in human form, he humbled himself and became obedient to the point of death – even death on a cross. *(Philippians 2:3-8)*

If anyone could have claimed to be special, it was Jesus! He alone could claim to be better than others, for he was without sin, the Son of God, able to offer eternal life, forgiveness of sins, reconciliation with God, everything anyone can ever need for fulfilment and happiness in life. Just imagine the sort of build-up he could have given himself to impress the crowds and win their support. And yet, throughout his life, we see only humility, putting himself last and others first, pointing away from himself to the Father, offering his life for the life of the world.

In the example of Jesus there is a challenge for us today. Are we like those advertisements, blowing our own trumpets, full of ourselves and our own importance – what we are, what we've done, what we want, what we know and what we think? Or are we ready to learn from Jesus and follow in his footsteps, taking the path of self-sacrifice and self-denial. Which way will we choose?

EASTER

13   A miraculous change!

Reading   John 11:25-6; 19:19-23

Aim   To illustrate the great transformation that Easter brought about in the life of the disciples and the life of the world.

Preparation   On pieces of card or paper, and in large, bold characters, write or print the following letters:

A A C D E E E E F H H I I I L M N N O R R R S T T T U

Attach a small piece of magnetic tape to the back of each, and arrange them on a board as follows:

ISNT THERE A MIRACLE HERE   FIND OUT

Talk   Read out the words displayed on the board, then ask the congregation if anyone can spot what the 'miracle' might be? Suggest that they might like to change things around to arrive at a very different message, reminding them of the words of Jesus in the reading shared earlier. When the right answer is given, or if it is clear no one is going to guess it, rearrange the letters on the board to spell out the following:

I AM THE RESURRECTION AND THE LIFE

From one message to another – an astonishing transformation, yet not half as astonishing as the miracle we celebrate today: the resurrection of Jesus Christ from the dead. To the disciples and followers of Jesus the events they had witnessed in the days leading up to Easter spoke only of death, tragedy, sorrow and disaster. There seemed nothing left to hope for, no reason to expect any change in their situation. They had watched Jesus suffer and die, then seen him buried in a tomb and the stone rolled against the entrance. The adventure of faith was over, and all their dreams with it.

But suddenly it was all turned around. Three women went to the tomb and came back with the news that Jesus was not there. Two men on the road to Emmaus declared that Jesus had met them on the way and broken bread with them. And then, as the disciples huddled together in the upper room, Jesus appeared amongst them, risen and victorious. It seemed too good to be true, but it wasn't – Jesus was alive!

'I am the resurrection and the life.' That's what Jesus told his followers. And that's what he tells us today. It is a miracle that some find difficult if not impossible to accept, and that many across the centuries have argued fiercely over. We can't prove it any more than they can, but we can find out the truth for ourselves, for the risen Christ is constantly waiting to meet with each one of us and transform our lives in turn. We need simply to respond, to put our trust in him and give him space to work. Do that, and we will find a miracle not just in the words of Scripture but deep within our hearts – life changed for ever!

14   Sense or nonsense?

Reading
Luke 24:1-12

Aim
To show that, while some may ridicule the idea of resurrection, to the eye of faith it is a truth that makes sense of everything.

Preparation
Display the following on a board:

$E = MC^2$

$2 = 2 = 5$

$4 \times 4 = 16$

$5 - 3 = 7$

Tfotf ps opotfotf

'Twas brillig and the slithy toves

$101 + 110 = 11$

Ring a ring of roses

All dogs are animals, therefore all animals are dogs

A bird in the hand is worth two in the bush

'emeism de kerussomen Xriston 'estauromenon

He is not here; he has risen

Talk
Tell the congregation you need their help to sort out some sense from nonsense. Taking each of the displayed statements in turn, ask whether they make any sense or not. After giving time for answers, make the following comments about each:

$E = MC^2$
We may not be able to understand this, but it is central to Einstein's theory of relativity.

$2 = 2 = 5$
This is clearly nonsense.

$4 \times 4 = 16$
This makes perfect sense.

$5 - 3 = 7$
This is clearly nonsense.

Tfotf ps opotfotf
This looks like nonsense, but in fact is code for 'Sense or nonsense' (A=B, B=C, C=D, etc.).

'Twas brillig and the slithy toves
These are the opening words of a nonsense poem by Lewis Carroll, but although the poem is nonsense it sounds like it makes sense!

101 + 110 = 11

This is nonsense using Arabic numbers, but perfect sense using
  binary numbers for the first part of the equation.

Ring a ring of roses
This dates back to the days of the Black Death.

All dogs are animals, therefore all animals are dogs
This sounds logical but, of course, is complete nonsense.

A bird in the hand is worth two in the bush
Taken literally this is nonsense, but the point this proverb is making
  makes good sense.

'emeism de kerussomen Xriston 'estauromenon
This may look like nonsense, but in fact is Greek for 'Yet we proclaim
  Christ crucified' *(1 Corinthians 1:23)*.

He is not here; he has risen
There are many who will tell us this is nonsense, but as Christians
  we believe it is true.

Some of the statements are nonsense, some look like nonsense but
in fact are good sense, some seem to make sense but are actually nonsense, and some make perfect sense as they stand. All of which goes
to show that making sense of something is not always as easy as we
might think. And if we still doubt that, let's look back to the reaction
of the disciples of Jesus when the women ran back from the tomb to
tell them that the tomb was empty and Jesus had risen:

> They did not believe the women, because their words seemed to
> them like nonsense. *(Luke 24:11)*

It wasn't that the disciples didn't want to believe; simply that for a
moment it seemed too good to be true. Only when they saw Jesus for
themselves were they finally fully convinced.

There are still, of course, many today who claim that the resurrection of Jesus is nonsense, that there is no way it could ever have
happened.

We cannot prove them wrong, any more than they can prove themselves right, for the truth of the resurrection can only be discovered
through personal experience. But when we open our lives to the reality of the risen Christ, then not only do we discover the truth about
resurrection; we discover a faith that makes sense of life itself.

15   An astonishing comeback!

Reading   Matthew 28:1-20

Aim   To bring home the awesome and astonishing truth of Jesus' resurrection from the dead.

Preparation   This talk focuses on people and places that have made surprising comebacks having been written off as past history, or having lost something of their past glory. Examples are given below, but these date quickly and you will need to add questions of your own, drawing on recent news (in the world of sport, pop music and cinema, for example). There is no need to prepare any visual material for the talk, though you may find it useful to display the names of places or people who have made an astonishing comeback.

- Which two countries were among the first to regain their identity from the old Soviet Union? (Latvia and Lithuania)

- Which heavy metal pop group split up several years ago but then reformed with old and new members? (Status Quo)

- Which Victorian garden has been carefully restored by the National Trust after years of neglect? (Biddulph Grange)

- Which Scottish TV series about a doctor was remade several years ago, many years after the original series? (Dr Finlay)

- What form of transport is running again in Manchester years after it was scrapped? (Tram)

- Which Royal home was badly damaged by fire several years ago but has now been fully restored? (Windsor Castle)

- What farm animal is once again a common sight, having nearly been lost to our country altogether? (Jacob sheep)

- Which Midlands city and cathedral was rebuilt after being almost totally destroyed during the Second World War? (Coventry)

- What famous feature of York Minster was lovingly remade, having been destroyed by fire? (Rose Window)

- Which football team plays at The Valley, having returned there after years away from the ground during which time the club almost became extinct? (Charlton Athletic)

- Which well-loved British boxer made numerous comebacks, finally becoming world heavyweight champion? (Frank Bruno)

Talk   Tell the congregation you have prepared a quiz about people, things and places that have made surprising comebacks.

Each of these people, things or places seemed for a time to have reached the end of their useful lives, either having finished their careers or having been so badly damaged as to be beyond repair. All were written off as belonging to the past, has-beens that had had their day, but all, in different ways, made unexpected comebacks, finding a new lease of life, each with a fascinating story to tell.

Yet none of those stories, extraordinary though they may be, are as amazing or wonderful as the event we celebrate today – the resurrection of Jesus! He too, like all of these, seemed to belong to the past. He was dead and buried, and, as far as his enemies were concerned, his life over. But, just in case, they took steps to ensure there was no way he could come back, dead or alive:

> The chief priests and the Pharisees gathered before Pilate and said, 'Sir, we remember what the imposter said while he was still alive, "After three days I will rise again." Therefore command the tomb to be made secure on the third day, otherwise his disciples may go and steal him away, and tell the people, "He has been raised from the dead," and the last deception will be worse than the first.' Pilate said to them, 'You have a guard of soldiers; go, make it as secure as you can.' So they went with the guard and made the tomb secure by sealing the stone. *(Matthew 27:62-66)*

Having done that, not only his enemies believed they could forget him; his friends thought so too. They believed it was all over, his life at an end, the only thing left to console them being memories of times past. But then Mary, Peter, and the rest of the disciples came to realise how mistaken they were.

> He is not here; for he has been raised, as he said. Come, see the place where he lay. *(Matthew 28:6)*

> They departed quickly from the tomb with fear and great joy, and ran to tell his disciples. And behold, Jesus met them.
> *(Matthew 28:8)*

Jesus had come back, just as he promised he would! He was alive! And not just picking up where he left off, but victorious over death and evil, returning to give new life to his followers!

There are many astonishing comebacks in the list we looked at earlier, comebacks that left those who witnessed them shaking their heads in astonishment, but none is anywhere near so amazing or half as wonderful as the resurrection of Christ that we celebrate today.

ASCENSION

16 The complete picture

Reading

Acts 1:6-11

Aim

To show that the Ascension has a vital place in the Christian Year, balancing the humanity of Christ with his divinity, and so offering a complete picture of God's revelation in Christ.

Preparation

First, on a large sheet of card, draw a simple picture, such as the one below, which can be interpreted in two ways – as a vase or as two faces. Display this on a board.

Now, on another large sheet of card, write exactly as written, in large print, the following numbers. (You may be able to print these if your word processor or computer has a similar font.)

738051
7108
7738
805
35007
7735
3807
7718
57108
5317
55378
5537
7105

Retain this list of numbers for use later in the talk.

Talk   Display the picture you have prepared and ask what people can see. Spend time drawing out a number of responses, and ensure that everybody is finally able to spot both of the ways the picture can be viewed. Bring out the fact that what we see depends on what we are looking for, and that it is very possible for us to see only half the picture.

Now display the list of numbers, and again ask people what they see. Run through the numbers one by one and invite people to confirm the numbers you have written. Ask if anyone can see anything different in what you have written. Turn the display over, and ask again. You should see the following: SOIL, LESS, BLESS, LIES, BOILS, BILL, LOBE, SELL, LOOSE, SOB, BELL, BOIL, ISOBEL.

These are two examples of the way that what we see depends on what we are looking for – examples that remind us how all too easily we can see only half a picture. And Ascension Day reminds us of exactly this truth. It is a day that recalls the departing of Jesus into heaven, lifted up suddenly into the clouds, but what we have here is figurative language used in an attempt to describe an indescribable moment. Precisely what happened we cannot be sure, but what matters is not the manner of Jesus' Ascension, but the truth behind it. And for the Apostles this meant that, for the first time in their lives, they saw the whole picture about Jesus, instead of simply a part. Until then, though they had seen him as the Messiah, revered him as a teacher, and worshipped him as the risen Lord, they had not fully grasped the fact that he was one with God. But at this moment, as he was taken from them, the truth dawned. In this man, who had walked beside them and whom they had followed for three extraordinary years, they had encountered not simply the Son of God, incredible though that was, but God himself, for Jesus and the Father were one.

And in turn the Ascension reminds us that Jesus was not only human like each of us, but also divine – wholly man yet wholly God. Lose sight of either of those truths, stress one at the cost of the other, and we will see only half the picture, missing out on the wonder of God's revelation in Christ.

PENTECOST

17 Symbols of the Spirit

Reading Acts 2:1-13

Aim To demonstrate that the symbols we used to describe our experience of the Holy Spirit each convey an important truth, but none can express what is finally beyond words.

Preparation Reproduce the weather symbols below.

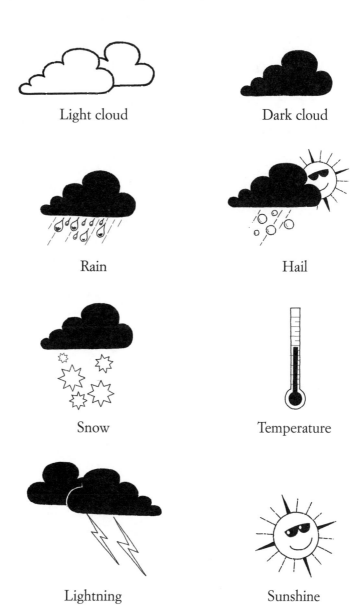

Light cloud

Dark cloud

Rain

Hail

Snow

Temperature

Lightning

Sunshine

Sunshine and showers

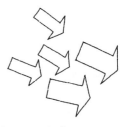

Gales

Talk   Explain that you want today to think about symbols, and to help you do that you are going to show them some of the symbols they see every day on the weather forecast. One by one, display the symbols you have prepared and ask if anybody can identify them.

With some of the symbols the meaning is obvious. We only have to look at them to tell straightaway what they mean. But other aspects of the weather, like, for example, wind, are more difficult to portray. It's the best symbol the weather forecasters have been able to come up with so far, and once you've seen it explained you know next time what it means. We cannot actually show what wind looks like any more than we can temperature.

And so it is with the Holy Spirit. We do not know what the Spirit looks like, where it is or what it is doing, but we experience it in our lives and need symbols to describe that experience. And the three most commonly used are the dove, a symbol of peace; wind, a symbol of power; and fire, a symbol of cleansing. Each points to one aspect of the Holy Spirit's work in our lives, but none of them, even when put together, can tell us the whole truth. These symbols help us glimpse the truth, but to understand it fully we need to experience the reality of the Spirit for ourselves.

18 Power for living

Readings Luke 24:44-49; Ephesians 3:14-21

Aim To bring home the fact that the Holy Spirit is the source of power for Christian faith and discipleship.

Preparation On separate pieces of card, write or print the following in large, bold characters:

gas	light
diesel	engine
steam	locomotive
hydroelectric	dam
horse	power
solar	panel
wave	barrage
petrol	pump
wind	mill
nuclear	reactor
oil	well
coal	mine

Arrange those in the first column down the left-hand side of a display board, and place the words in the second column randomly on the right-hand side, taking care not to form a matching pair.

Talk Ask the congregation what all the words in the left column on the display have in common (they are all forms of power). Invite suggestions as to which of the words on the right match those on the left (note that 'engine' and 'locomotive' fit with both 'diesel' and 'steam'). As each answer is given insert this next to its matching pair (as above).

These are just some of the forms of power we depend upon in our daily lives, and if any were to run out we would soon notice the difference. So great is our demand for power that one of the great quests of our modern age is to discover an unlimited source of renewable energy.

But for us as Christians there is one source of power more important than all of these, and that is the power first promised by Jesus to his disciples at the end of his earthly ministry:

See, I am sending upon you what my Father promised; so stay here in the city until you have been clothed with power from on high. *(Luke 24:49)*

This was the power of the Holy Spirit which was to come suddenly and unexpectedly upon the Apostles on the day of Pentecost, transforming them from uncertain and fearful believers to fearless ambassadors for Christ. And it is that same power which is promised to us and each and every believer. In the words of the Apostle Paul:

> I pray that, according to the riches of his glory, he may grant that you may be strengthened in your inner being with power through his Spirit. *(Ephesians 3:16)*

Whoever we are, however weak or powerless we may feel, God, through his Holy Spirit, is able to take us and use us in ways beyond any we can ever imagine. That is the promise Pentecost reminds us of year by year: God's gift of power for living!